SO-BXI-815

MISSIONARY MIRACLES

COMPILED BY

CHRIS STEWART

WITH JOHN CROWLEY

DESERET
BOOK

© 2009 The Shipley Group

All rights reserved. No part of this book may be reproduced in any form or by any means without permission in writing from the publisher, Deseret Book Company, P. O. Box 30178, Salt Lake City, Utah 84130. This work is not an official publication of The Church of Jesus Christ of Latter-day Saints. The views expressed herein are the responsibility of the author and do not necessarily represent the position of the Church or of Deseret Book Company.

DESERET BOOK is a registered trademark of Deseret Book Company.

Visit us at DeseretBook.com

Library of Congress Cataloging-in-Publication Data

Missionary miracles : stories and letters from the field / Chris Stewart, compiler.
    p. cm.
    ISBN 978-1-59038-749-8 (pbk.)
    1. Missionary stories.   2. Mormon missionaries.   3. Church of Jesus Christ of Latter-day Saints—Missions.   I. Stewart, Chris, 1960–
    BV2087.M57 2008
    266'.9332—dc22   2008012446

Printed in the United States of America
Worzalla Publishing Co., Stevens Point, WI

10   9   8   7   6   5   4   3   2   1

Contents

CONTENTS

Introduction

As anyone who has ever known a full-time missionary will tell you, there is nothing quite like the e-mails and letters the young men and women send home, and receiving them is the highlight of the week for parents and family members.

This volume brings together many of these unique "epistles" from missionaries, serving in places as far-flung as Madagascar, Russia, South America, South Africa, and the United States. (Names of missionary companions and contacts have been changed to preserve their privacy.) In the letters, the elders and sisters provide vivid descriptions of the cultures in which they are living, the lessons they are learning, their homesickness, and the miraculous experiences they are having. More important, they share their love of the work as they labor as ambassadors of the Lord Jesus Christ.

Filled with expressions of love and faith, these testimonies explain why our youth grow up singing "I hope they call me on a mission," and will serve also to inspire readers and encourage other young people to prepare themselves for one of the greatest spiritual adventures they could ever have.

PART 1

THE EFFECTS OF
THE GOSPEL

"And my soul shall be joyful in the Lord."
—Psalm 35:9

One of the great blessings a missionary experiences is seeing firsthand the change the gospel can make in the heart of someone who embraces it. Here missionaries share experiences that show how people grow when they accept the gospel light.

1

"The Best Day I've Had"

LISA ERICKSON
Brazil Belo Horizonte Mission

Fam,

This last week was truly a great one. Things have been pretty frustrating the last little while, so we had a meeting with the elders in our ward about how we can turn this place around. Our meeting ended with a desperate prayer to our Heavenly Father to help us and guide us to be able to help this ward grow.

I think the next day was the best day I've had on my mission so far. We went out to the "end of the world" for a couple of discussions with families there. The first discussion was with a family we've been teaching for a few months. The mother has a testimony and wants to be baptized, but the father has been very hard-hearted because of their financial problems and thinks that God has abandoned him.

They also have had problems with their marriage due to the financial stress. The father had to go to work for his father—four hours away on foot, in the middle of nowhere. When we got to their home, he had returned from work as a completely different person. He told us that he now trusts God and has faith that God knows what's best for his family.

After that we went to our next appointment. The husband has already heard the discussions twice and has really changed but always has some excuse not to be baptized. Right now his excuse is that he doesn't know how to pray correctly, even though he has a testimony and goes to church every week. We gave a lesson about the Savior's sacrifice and asked him to choose someone to pray for us. He hesitated, and his wife asked him again to choose someone. He turned to us and asked if he could say the prayer. We quickly agreed and bowed our heads before he could change his mind. It was a beautiful prayer. He cried, his wife cried, we cried, everyone hugged, and we left in complete awe of the spirit we had felt.

Well, if that wasn't enough for one day, we had planned to visit a family who had been taught by

some other missionaries but hadn't yet been baptized. When we got there they were excited to see us.
The mother cried as she told us that she had been
praying for God to send us to them.

My companion and I couldn't do a thing after
that. We just sat by the edge of a dirt road at the
"end of the world" for about thirty minutes and
thanked our Heavenly Father for the changes we had
seen. Everyone always asks if we ever get homesick—
yes, I miss you all, but I feel like the luckiest person
in the world to be here and to be able to witness so
many miracles, even something as simple as a prayer.
Don't ever doubt it; don't ever forget it.

Love you,
Lisa

2

"'God Will Tell Me'"

ADAM BECKSTRAND HESS

Utah Ogden Mission

Dear Mom and Dad,

The Lord blessed me with another wonderful experience two weeks ago, the fruits of which I witnessed last night at the baptism of Matt Horton. My companion and I had finished most of our work in the office, so we decided to get out and try to lose ourselves in the work. The second house we knocked on literally slammed the door in our faces. The next door we were greeted by a woman who invited us in. She was a member of the Church and said her husband wasn't home yet but that her eighteen-year-old son had just returned home from Las Vegas about two weeks before and was living with them. At that moment her son, Matt, came running up the stairs with the Bible in his hand, opened to a verse. He was so excited he was literally out of breath as he explained that the Lord had just answered his prayers through a verse in the Bible.

He went on to tell us how he had left home at the age of thirteen and had spent the next five years in Las Vegas, on drugs, having turned his back on God. He had expected to die there on the streets of Las Vegas, but he had had a spiritual experience too sacred to share and through that was led home with a determination to repair his relationship with his family and find out what God would have him do. We later found out that just before we knocked, he had been praying for strength and how to find it. We could feel the Spirit as he talked; he was like a little kid, bubbling with enthusiasm over something he had learned for the first time. Matt told us he wanted us to teach him everything we knew. We smiled and said we would.

The whole family gathered in the living room, and we taught them the first discussion. It was Mom and Dad and Matt's two younger sisters, all of whom had been baptized. The look of wonder in their eyes as they watched their son and brother speak of the

Spirit and the change in his heart was enough to make you cry. We taught Matt about Joseph Smith and how he had many of the same questions Matt had. We shared the First Vision with him and asked how he could find out for himself that it really happened. "God will tell me," he said. Elder Jones and I testified that God would tell him as he prayed to know. We knelt with them as a family, and as each of us prayed that Matt would receive an answer to his prayers, the Spirit was poured out upon us. Matt offered the last prayer, and his voice trembled as the Holy Ghost testified to him of the reality of Joseph Smith's experience. There were tears in every eye as Elder Jones invited Matt to follow his answer and be baptized two weeks from that day. He exclaimed "Yes!" and jumped to his feet and hugged us both, thanking us for finding him. Matt had returned to the Lord, and his family was reunited with their son and brother. What a privilege it is to be a small part in the greatest work in the world.

Love,
Elder Adam Beckstrand Hess

3

"She'd Never Felt So Happy"

ALISON BOULTER

Wisconsin Milwaukee Mission

Hey there, Mom and Dad!

Man, I have lots to tell you! What an interesting week we have had! The past two days in particular. Yesterday, the Fourth of July, we went to church, and it was really nice. Rose, our eighty-one-year-old investigator, came and had a good time. She cries all through church, and, watching her, I can hardly keep the tears back myself. She is amazing. I love her! I swear I knew her in the preexistence.

I wanted to tell you the most amazing story that I will probably tell from my mission. It is about a lady named Jessie. Jessie had investigated the Church about four years ago, but one of the elders said something offensive to her, and she didn't want anything to do with the Church after that. Well, we had "referral week" in the mission back in May, and we hit up the members for anyone they knew that we might teach. We got twelve referrals from the ward! That in itself was a miracle. One of the sisters referred her neighbor (Jessie) because she knew she had investigated a long time ago. We chose a day to be in the neighborhood and knocked on her door. She came to the door pretty flustered and told us to come back the following Friday. We did, and she let us in. She seemed really nervous and anxious with us there, and the appointment didn't last long, but we did make sure we told her that God loved her. She has gone through more trials than anyone I have ever met. We set up another appointment for the next week.

We met with her on a regular basis, a couple times a week for two months. We watched her as she grew to love the Book of Mormon. We saw how it helped her quit smoking and drinking coffee, and finally she told us she wanted to be baptized. She was baptized last week. Her baptism was incredible. There wasn't a dry eye in the room.

The night after she was baptized, our phone

rang. It was Jessie. I asked how she felt and she said she'd never felt so happy or so comfortable with life. Then she told me something that I couldn't believe. She said that the first day we met with her, she had had two agendas. The first was to tell us, politely, of course, that she would never join the Church. The second was that she was planning on committing suicide that night. She had everything planned and was all ready to go. She said that after meeting with us, she figured she could hold out for a few more days. After each meeting, she felt she could hold on longer, until the thoughts of suicide completely left her. I couldn't believe what I was hearing. It strengthened my testimony so much of the Lord's timing and of how well He knows each of His children.

I am so thankful that I have been able to have these experiences. Missionary work really is a privilege.

I love you!
Sister Boulter

4

"I Can See Such a Huge Difference"

BRENDA MALONE

Madagascar Antananarivo Mission

Background: Madagascar is a third-world country, located on a big, tropical island in the Indian Ocean. Malagasy is their native tongue, though some French is spoken. The Church is very new there, the first LDS full-time missionaries having come only about twelve years ago. It is a dirty, dusty, but beautiful place where the Church is advancing very well. The following includes five stories from letters showing the conversion of one of the Malagasy people.

April 5

Soeur Smith and I were a little late to an appointment, but she decided that we should finish knocking on the rest of the doors on the street. Rufin's door was the last one on the street. Had I been in charge, I'm sure I would have just said, "Let's come back later; we need to get to our appointment." But we knocked on his door. He let us in, we taught him a first discussion, and he came to church the next day. Yesterday, he was baptized! (Incidentally, we still made it to that appointment we were late for, so it really all worked out well!)

June 7

Guess what? Do you remember Rufin, the young man Soeur Smith and I taught who was baptized a couple of months ago? Well, he's serving as a mini-missionary now! There aren't enough full-time missionaries, so he's been called to serve until a replacement comes. Isn't that great? I couldn't be prouder. He's a great missionary; I just know it. He's always so happy. His favorite things to say are, *"Mahafinaritra be!"* and *"Tsara be!"* basically meaning, "That's great!"

August 2

After the concert on Friday, Rufin asked to speak to me and Soeur Smith in private. He wanted to express his gratitude that we'd come to his house and shared the gospel with him. He said the most wonderful things to us—that his life had taken a huge turnaround, that perhaps he wouldn't even be alive right now were it not for the gospel, and that he would never, ever forget us. He recently found out that he's twenty-six years old (up until a week ago, he had no idea how old he was; it turns out his birthday is a day after mine!), and he's really upset that he can't serve a mission himself, but he wants to continue to serve mini-missions, like the one he just finished before the last transfer.

It was just wonderful to hear his words. It struck me how we really weren't the ones who gave him this happiness. We were just going out and doing what missionaries do. It was he that was ready. How grateful I am, though, that Soeur Smith and I were able to be instruments in the Lord's hands to help him! Rufin bore his testimony on Sunday. I'm so proud of him! I'm really lucky to get to see some of the fruits of our efforts here while I'm in the field.

September 27

This week I've had the choice experience of working with one of our ward missionaries, Rufin

Randriana, the young man I taught with Soeur Smith who was baptized in April. It has been the sweetest joy I've ever had to work with him! He's now shared his conversion story twice with some of our investigators, mentioning that I was the missionary who had come to his door and shared the gospel with him. I remember well that he came to church the day after we first taught him—we were floored! I was surprised to hear him say while telling his conversion story the other day that he'd had no intention of going that Sunday. But then he followed our invitation to read a little from the Book of Mormon. It touched his heart, and he came.

Even in the short time I've known him, I can see such a huge difference in who he has become since he was introduced to the gospel. He used to be (and he fully admits this) something of a "gangster type." So he has a rather disarrayed past, but now he is a rock-solid member of the true Church of God, not the least bit ashamed of the gospel of Christ. Before, he was timid, shy, quiet, and didn't smile much. Now I hardly ever see him not smiling! He makes me so happy!

I'll always have a special place in my heart for him. What a privilege it is for me to get to work with him. All of the other missionaries just love him, too. Whenever they talk about how great he is, I just beam with pride. He's currently working at the main Church building here in Tana, planting flowers and tending the grounds. He takes such pride in his work. When we go to work with him, he often comments on the beautiful shrubbery he sees, or he'll tell us the proper ways to take care of plants.

March 14

Rufin is getting married this week!!!!!!! He's been dating a girl for a long time, but I had no idea that they were that serious! She just got baptized a few weeks ago. Her name is Nekena, and I'm really excited for him. They won't have a ceremony or anything—just the paper signing. And it's supposed to be secret until the signing is over this Thursday. Then we can tell people! He says that his next goal is to go to the temple. He has very little money, but he is full of faith. I love how much the gospel has changed his life.

5

"A Miracle Right before Our Eyes"

JAMES CROWLEY
Mission unidentified

Dear Mom and Dad and Family,

Yesterday was amazing. We were walking to an appointment when I remembered that we had Sandra White marked for an eight o'clock appointment and that we needed to get a woman from the ward to testify to her. Sandra has been to church two times with her son and her daughters, and we had tried everything to help her make the decision to be baptized, but she always responded that she first needed an answer to her prayers. It was really frustrating because she had accepted everything and knew that it was right. She and her family had read the Book of Mormon like none other, and she told us that she loved the Church.

So the other day we were inspired that we

needed to take some of the women of the ward there to testify. We ran to Brother Sterling's house and asked if his wife could go with us, but she wasn't able to. Then we called the bishop's wife, but she couldn't go either. Finally we called Sister Fletcher, and she said she would go.

We met her at a bakery and began walking together to Sandra's house and explaining the situation. As we were walking, Sister Fletcher asked if we had thought of her when we knew that we needed to take someone to visit Sandra. When we said we had, she said, "That's perfect." When we asked why, she said we would see why while we were at Sandra's house.

As we were walking, I began to pray in my heart that God would tell us which message we should teach and also that Sister Fletcher would be an instrument in God's hands to touch Sandra's heart and help her decide to be baptized.

In very little time we arrived at Sandra's house. She was there with her elderly mother, who lives with her. We went in and visited a little while; then we asked if we could leave a message with her. She agreed, and Elder Todd asked if I had my *palestras* [discussions] and I answered that I did. Then he explained to Sandra that it was marked to teach the fourth *palestra* but that we would teach the third again instead. This was a surprise to me, because we had already taught her the third discussion twice, and she hadn't accepted the Church as the only true church. The second time we taught it, we used many of the scriptures in the Bible to testify, but she still hadn't accepted the concept and hadn't agreed to be baptized.

So this was the third time. And this time I taught the first two principles almost word for word, using many scriptures again. Then Elder Todd taught the third and fourth principles and read the *palestra* to her word for word. Then he asked Sister Fletcher to tell us how she felt about the Church and to describe the blessings she had received as a result of her membership.

Sister Fletcher started testifying and describing a dream she had recently had. As she did, she began to cry. And Sandra began to talk with her and explain her feelings, and then Sister Fletcher testified again.

This exchange went on for about ten to fifteen minutes.

Then it was my turn to teach about living prophets, and I read the fifth principle word for word. After I had finished, I asked Sandra if she accepted this church as the only true church on the face of the whole earth.

And she said, "Yes!"

As I congratulated her, I was almost crying as well. And when she turned to shake Elder Todd's hand, he too was dumbfounded. He had been praying through the *palestra* that God would touch her heart, and when she said yes, he almost fainted and was in a little bit of shock. But he quickly snapped out of it and shook her hand.

I asked her how she had reached that conclusion, and she said that it was because of what Sister Fletcher had said to her. She said it was as if she had heard those exact words before.

When she said that, I did begin to cry, and I knew that my prayer had been answered!

I then asked her if she would follow those feelings and be baptized. She said she would, and she and her kids will be baptized on the twentieth of August.

It was a miracle that happened right before our eyes. That experience taught us with such power that God hears and answers our prayers. This work is His and has nothing to do with us. He has the power to touch people's hearts and help them see the spiritual things. It also taught us that it is a huge privilege to serve Him and learn more about His power and love. And to realize the potential that we all have.

I love this work. It is humbling and amazing.

I love you all,
James

6

"He Calls Us His *Angelitas*"

REBECCA WAREHAM

Spain Barcelona Mission

Background note from Sister Wareham's mother: My daughter was in her second transfer in the mission, still struggling to learn Spanish, and learning what it means to be a missionary. She prefaced every letter by saying, "Has this been the best week ever, or what?" I think this one really was.

Hola, familia!!!

Has this been the best week ever, or what???? Yes, it definitely has!!! At the beginning of this month, we started teaching a man named Sergio, whose daughter, Alba, is a member. When I first met him, I was thinking there was no way we could teach him because he didn't want to listen to two dumb American girls. Plus he was waaaay Catholic. Our first *charla* was mostly him yelling at us, and we didn't really get much done. I left thinking, *Hmm, his daughter is nuts if she thinks we can convert him.*

Well, Alba has more faith than anyone I've ever met in my life, and she wouldn't let us give up on Sergio. So we kept teaching him, and each time he listened a little more and seemed to be a little more willing to make commitments. During the second charla, we found out that he had some pretty serious concerns about past transgressions and familial issues. He didn't think he could be forgiven.

It was incredible how the *charla* went. Hermana Salazar passed the ball to me a little unexpectedly, and somehow I ended up giving my testimony about how the Atonement has worked in my life. From that moment on, we didn't have any problems with Sergio.

He listened intently to every word we said, he read everything we asked him to, he prayed, and he even gave up coffee. And now he's getting baptized this weekend. It is so amazing!!!!!!!!!!!! He calls us his *angelitas* for bringing him the gospel, but we really didn't do anything.

Every day I realize that. We do so little, but

receive so many blessings! It's so contrary to everything I thought about missions. I came out here with this idea of, "Yeah, look at me, I'm going to serve the Lord for eighteen months, and I'm going to be obedient and work hard, and yeah, look at me sacrifice." It's not like that at all. The Lord is blessing me far beyond anything I'm giving.

People say that Europe is a tough place to convert, but I don't buy into that. We have three baptisms scheduled in the next three weeks, with another investigator who is going to be setting a *meta* soon. Every day we talk to incredible people who put their faith in God and are trying to be good people. I know the Lord is blessing us with success here and will continue to do so. Every week I marvel over how packed our schedule is. I love how busy we are!!! It's great!!! Spain is the best!!!

I love you!!!
Rebecca

7

"He Loves the Missionaries"

AUTHOR'S NAME WITHHELD
Korea Taejon Mission

Hello, family, how is everyone?

I had kind of a great experience yesterday. Well, it wasn't really a great experience, but I learned a great lesson. You see, there is a man in our ward named Brother Su, and he is just a little strange. Socially, he is not the smartest person, and he can be really mean and sometimes weird. Still, he loves the missionaries. He loves them so much and respects them with respect that I know I don't deserve. It's kind of sad because he has no friends outside of the missionaries. On his birthday, he even bought his own cake and invited us to eat it with him, so he wouldn't have to spend his day alone. In doing so, he spent too much and didn't have enough bus money, so he had to walk fifteen miles to his house in Kimje. (I think it might actually be more than fifteen miles; it takes one hour by bus.)

Yesterday after English class, we went out to eat with him and some other members. On the way to dinner, we were approached by a beggar who said he was hungry and asked us for some money. We told him we couldn't give him money but said that he could come eat with us and we would buy him a dinner. It was so sad to see this man and his condition and his clothes. He smelled awful, and he told us he was homeless and had no place to shower—that he had been in a car wreck that left him badly injured. Before that he had been normal, but now he is unable to think properly and hasn't been able to get a job. It was sad.

After dinner, as we were saying good-bye, the man asked us for money again, and Brother Su gave him a few bucks. Then we took a taxi to our house, and when we got there, Brother Su got out with us. Normally, he would have stayed in the taxi and ridden it to the bus terminal. But he got out and said he was going to walk home. I thought he didn't have the money for the bus, so we tried to give him ten bucks, but he wouldn't take it. So we dropped it on the ground and ran into our apartment building. He ran after us and caught us before we could get inside our door. He was crying, saying how sorry he felt for the beggar. Brother Su said that he had money, and yet he didn't give more than a few bucks. He explained that if he had given more, he would have had to walk the fifteen or twenty miles home. Now he was mad at himself for being so selfish and said he just couldn't ride a bus home, because he felt as if the money wasn't his. He should have given it to the man.

Then he talked about all the blessings he had found in the gospel, the love of his Heavenly Father and his Savior, and that this beggar had none of these things. He talked about how when he was walking home the week before, all he could think about was how grateful he was to God for all the things He had given him. I learned such a great lesson, watching this twenty-eight-year-old man, without a friend in the world, crying because he hadn't helped someone when he could have and expressing his gratitude for the blessings of the gospel.

It was also amazing to me that as he talked, for whatever reason, all of his physical problems were temporarily gone. His stutter was gone, the weird thing he does with his eyes and mouth was gone. All of the things that cause him to struggle socially, problems that I can't fully describe, were gone. And it wasn't just that I didn't notice them—they were actually not there. It was an amazing transformation to me. Almost a miracle. Maybe it happened so I could learn a lesson or something, but I looked at him and he was a normal person, just like anyone else.

One of the elders later pointed out that that's how Brother Su is going to be in the resurrection. And I thought about how someday I will see him and the others like him whom I have met and haven't treated with kindness, or those whom I wasn't mean to but maybe just ignored, and they might be crying then, too, just like Brother Su was last night, thanking me for my friendship, or crying, asking me why I treated them the way I had or why I had refused to be their friend.

I learned two great lessons, and it humbled me greatly.

Well, I have to go now. It's lunchtime, so maybe we will have some kimchi stew. Sounds good, huh?

I love you and miss you all,
(name withheld)

8

"It Put Her at Ease"

MAX HALL
Iowa Des Moines Mission

Dear Mom,

I have to start out by telling you a funny story about Sister Norton's baptism and how even though it was embarrassing for me, it was inspired.

I was in the bathroom getting changed into my whites. As I'm doing this Sister Norton is having a really hard time. I guess she was scared of the water or maybe the whole idea of commitment. So she was in the bishop's office getting a blessing. And I'm kind of stressing out and praying that she will be able to make it through. After I finished changing clothes, I said a prayer in the bathroom.

When I opened my eyes from the prayer the first thing I saw was my big toe. My toenail was painted bright red! I had forgotten that right before I left

Cedar Rapids, I had gone to say good-bye to the Nortons, and their young daughter had painted my toenail bright red! (It was P-day and I was in sandals.) And of course when you baptize you are barefoot, and I didn't know what to do! So I decided I would cover it everywhere I went with my other foot.

I went out and sat in the foyer, covering my toe and waiting for Sis. Norton to come out. The bishop came out first and told me I needed to help get her mind off her fear of the water and calm her down. She came and sat next to me and was literally shaking. She was basically freaking out, and nothing I said to her made any difference.

But then I had an idea! "Hey, Sister Norton. Wanna see something pretty embarrassing?" Then I showed her my toenail, which her daughter had painted. And you can probably guess what happened next. She busts up laughing at me. It totally calmed her down and put her at ease! She started making fun of me and stuff.

Then my ward mission leader walks by and sees my toe. "Elder! What is that?!" He puts his hand on his forehead and just starts shaking his head. Then the bishop walks up and asks, "What happened there, Elder?" He was laughing and also thought it was funny. But I'm sitting there stressing out! I can't walk in there with my toe like this!

Bro. Norton said, "Stay here, I'll be right back." Three minutes later he came back with a Band-Aid to put over my toenail. I felt a lot better, and Sister Norton was still laughing at me. So then we went into the Relief Society room for the service. When we sat down, she started getting real fidgety again. But I got her to sing the opening hymn with me. As we sang, the Spirit filled the room. It was incredibly strong. We sang "How Great Thou Art." Sister Norton stopped shaking and everything went perfectly after that.

Since her baptism she has been doing awesome. She loves church and has a very strong testimony. I am so happy I was able to help her.

Max

PART 2

A LEARNING EXPERIENCE

*"His lord said unto him, Well done, thou good
and faithful servant: thou hast been faithful . . .
enter thou into the joy of thy lord."*
—*Matthew 25:21*

It is often suggested that the first convert a missionary makes is himself or herself. These stories demonstrate the effects of a mission on the growth of the person serving it.

9

"It Was the Spirit"

JAMES M. JACKSON
Mission unidentified

Dear Family,

The Spirit was strong [in the MTC], but I was a little unsure of the strength of my testimony. I saw the new video of Joseph Smith and the Restoration. That movie touched me deeply. I knew it was true, although deep inside I still felt as though I had a weak testimony.

There was a devotional tonight, and Elder Merrill J. Bateman talked to all of us. This was an awesome talk! It primarily focused on *Preach My Gospel* and everything that has to do with it. The presence of the Spirit was so strong during the devotional. As I was sitting there the most amazing thing happened. All week I have felt as though my testimony was not strong enough to be a missionary. But after watching the video of the Restoration and feeling the Spirit as I watched it, I felt for certain that everything is true.

Throughout the week, hearing the other missionaries bear their testimonies, I have learned how to recognize the Spirit. But the most amazing thing was when I was listening to Elder Bateman speak to me. I was sitting there in my seat and felt something I have never felt before! I felt the Spirit testifying to me and telling me that the gospel of Jesus Christ is true and that I am serving a mission at this time because I have been chosen to do so. It was the Spirit that witnessed this to me—not another teacher, bishop, elder, parent, or friend. I know it was the Holy Ghost, in answer to my prayers, to help me know for sure that I am here for a reason. I know for a fact that this Church is true.

Your missionary son,
Elder James M. Jackson

10

"I Feel the Sun"

BRIAN THOMAS CLAY
Mexico Puebla Mission

Dear Family,

I have decided that things may not get easier. In fact, each week has been harder in some new and fascinating way than the last. I'm okay with that because it's all worth it. The question now becomes, What am I going to do about it? Am I going to let the clouds ruin my life?

Last week I was homesick for the first time since I left. I couldn't eat; I couldn't sleep; I was a wreck. But every day I got up and did what I was supposed to, and every day I prayed for more help. At one point, I didn't know what I was even doing here, but I knew that the sun is going to come out tomorrow. Here is the thing—it might only come out for a few seconds, so you better be ready to let its rays fall down on your face and warm your spirit.

When I'm with the families we teach, and I hear the prayer of an eight-year-old with a spirit and wisdom of someone well beyond her years, I feel the sun upon my face.

When we go to teach a family, and little Jorge runs up to me and takes me by the hand, when he sits on my lap through the lesson, playing with my tie and trying to climb up me like Mount Everest, I feel the sun on my back.

When we are able to lay our hands upon an investigator's head to confirm him a member of the Church and confer on him the gift of the Holy Ghost, I feel the "Son" in my heart.

These moments are the moments that will stand in my memory for years to come. They are the moments when every trial and difficulty of the mission fades into the background, and I feel the Son all around me.

I was thinking this week, Why do we stare at the stars? Why am I so enthralled by them? This is my answer: As I stare up into the vastness that is space, I am overwhelmed by its enormity. It stretches forever. How dark it would be without those points of light glimmering out there, calling me home. Those stars represent something to me. They represent hope. They let me know there is more out there—there is light; there is love; there is truth. Those lights are you, my family. They are my friends; they are the gospel; they are truth and hope; they are Christ.

Elder Clay

11

"I Felt an Overwhelming Joy"

NATHAN KEVIN ROBERTS
Mission unidentified

Dear Family,

Well, the other night I had a huge spiritual experience. I had this feeling as I was looking at a picture of Jesus Christ that I was responsible for causing His pain. I sat there and cried my eyes out for about twenty minutes. And then the next time I looked at the picture, I felt an overwhelming joy that I knew I had been forgiven of my sins, and I felt so happy; so I sent you each a bookmark with a picture of the Savior so that you can see His loving face. I hope all is well. I love you all. God bless.

Love,
Elder Roberts

12

"The Young People Hold Strong"

SARA HEILBUT

Finland Helsinki Mission

Rakkaat Perhe!

Saturday was my birthday! Yea! Sister Larson sang to me in the morning, and yes, I opened my present at 7:11, just like at home. It was way sweet. And then off to tract. That night was way fun! We went to the mission home, where Sister Johanson cooked me a birthday dinner! The elders came too. We talked, enjoyed her wonderful chicken with something and grapes, and President's homemade mashed potatoes! So good. Then they got the cake (cupcakes for everyone) ready and brought it in, and I started to giggle like a little girl, and Elder Johanson said, "Sister, you've been on a mission too long!" It was really funny. The president's wife put her arm around me and just gave me a hug, and the elders gave a great spiritual thought.

So it was a great day. I felt love from everyone around me and everyone at home as well.

Then there was Sunday! It was an amazing experience. The ward had a temple trip this weekend, and the members got back halfway through church, which is why we had sacrament meeting last. They decided just to have another testimony meeting for those to testify about the trip. I was overwhelmed. It is such a sacrifice for them to go. It took all weekend to go for one day. As they came back by boat, they had waves that were thirteen meters high, and didn't know how safe they were for a while. But person after person stood up and bore amazing testimony about how they love the temple. More amazing were the youth. One boy, sixteen years old, stood up right away and bore an amazing testimony that he loves the feelings at the temple and of how grateful he was to be able to go. Then another fifteen-year-old boy stood at the pulpit and told how at the last minute he put everything else aside and went, and as he testified that the temple is *"upea,"* he started to cry. I was overcome with how well these youth could get up there and bear a powerful testimony.

They had a youth conference the weekend

before, and our mission president and his wife said that the testimony meeting there was the same—full of strong testimonies of our Savior and of this gospel. Then something happened that really touched my heart. One girl got up who was only eleven years old and explained that even though she couldn't go into the temple yet and had waited in the nursery, she knew that the temple is the house of the Lord and said that she couldn't wait for the next year when she will be able to go in and fully participate.

After all this, I didn't want sacrament meeting to end. I saw the love in each member's eyes, from eleven- to sixty- or seventy-year-olds, and listened to them say how grateful they were that they had had the opportunity to go. It really touched me. I can't explain exactly how I felt, other than to say I experienced a renewed love for not only the Finns but also for the members in the ward and the members throughout the world, who don't have a temple five minutes down the road and who save all year to go once.

I also felt a love for the youth and received a strong testimony that they are the future and that is why we need to find them. I really love the youth of

Finland. They are so humble, willing, and eager to know. They are truly pioneers and stick to their values through thick and thin, in a land where for most people drinking is always the answer. Yet the young people hold strong and have a love for the Church I have never before seen. It made me grateful also for the opportunity I have had to live in an area with so many temples, with so many people who love me and who accept my values, without looking down on me or thinking I'm stupid. Truly, America is the promised land, and I know that more now than ever.

How lucky I am to have been born there and to be able to enjoy my religion as I please and have it actually mean something, and not just be a tradition—like opening presents at 7:11 in the morning on my birthday.

Being in that meeting and hearing those sweet testimonies truly humbled me, and I will never forget the feelings that I had. I left there with a renewed desire to serve and a greater love for these wonderful people. That was definitely the highlight of my week.

Have a great week yourselves. *Min rakastan teit!*

Sara

13

"We Should Make Him Cookies"

BRENDA MALONE

Madagascar Antananarivo Mission

Dear Family,

The happiest moment of the week for me . . . wasn't all of our opportunities to teach, wonderful as those were. I haven't as yet told you much about my thoughts regarding the poverty here in Madagascar. There are some people here who are very well off; they live in huge houses and have servants. Then there are people who live in modest homes, small but clean and adequate for their needs. Many of the poorest people live in huts and have no electricity, but we seldom visit them; we are, of course, friendly to them, but they aren't who we've been called to teach at this time (this is due to a principle called the Foundation Principle that was practiced at the beginning of my mission). They seem very happy, despite how little they have of worldly possessions. Finally, there are many who live on the streets, especially in the down-town area where there are the most tourists. Soeur Smith's and my area is far from downtown; and we aren't allowed to give money to beggars, at least not from our mission allotment. It is hard to see them begging yet feel helpless to do anything for them.

However, there are still a few beggars in our area. One of them is a little old deaf man, always smiling! He waves at us as we walk by, and we often go over to him and shake his hand. (I've learned, by the way, to avoid touching my face with all of the hand shaking we do around here!) I just love seeing him! There is also another beggar that we often see. He, unlike our deaf friend, always appears to be among the most mis-erable people I've ever seen. He looks so sad and in want! He has a mental disability of some kind; he is unable to speak and can only grunt. Occasionally, he approaches us, pointing to our bags and groaning. We, of course, have only scriptures in our bags and can never give him anything that would help him. One day after he did this, Soeur Smith said, "We should make him cookies sometime!" The Spirit always mo-tivates to action, and as she said this, I felt motivated!

So this week, during one of our lunch breaks, I

whipped up some oatmeal cookies and divided most of them into two bags. We gave one of the bags to our deaf friend that afternoon, and he received them with a friendly *"Misaotra!"* (Thank you!) The next day, I was happy when we saw our other beggar friend along the street, leaning up against the wall of a small store. He saw us approaching, and I think it scared him; he pointed to his left, groaning and indicating that he wanted us to leave. Then the most wonderful thing happened: I handed him the bag of cookies, and I'll never forget his reaction! His miserable, dirty face broke into a radiant smile, and he took the bag quickly from my hand. He tried to salute us in gratitude as he plopped himself down on the ground and started to open his treasure. Soeur Smith and I looked back at him moments later and waved at him; he looked back after us, still grinning from ear to ear. It just made my heart melt! We can't, of course, do this for him every day. But at least he knows, that at least for a moment, someone cares about him. And we definitely plan on making cookies for him again.

14

"Ten Things I Wish I'd Done"

CORTNEY LEE MATHEWS

Belgium Brussels/Netherlands Mission

Background: This letter was addressed to the members of the priests quorum in Elder Mathews's home ward.

Bonjour, my brethren:

As I sit here at my apartment in Belgium ending one cool P-day, I thought I'd be obedient in fulfilling a request of my dad! He asked me to make a list of ten things I could have, would have, or wished I would have done before my mission to better prepare myself! So . . . I'm gonna give it a shot:

1. Read the standard works over a few times, especially the Book of Mormon. I know you're all going to seminary, but reading a set number of pages is not good enough! I wish I would have read the

Book of Mormon 100 times over and had a better understanding of the scriptures all together.

2. Don't be alone with girls. I don't care how cute their "cooties" may be, taking the risk of being alone is not worth it at all! How much more fun (and safe) are group dates anyway?

3. Speak in church! Since being out here, I've given talks in conferences, meetings with missionaries/members, and many other meetings, in both French and English! Communication skills are really important, whether you're speaking English, Dutch, or Gibberish! (I'm actually fluent in Gibberish.) Ask the bishop and even our dear stake president, and they can hook you up each month with members of the high council.

4. Work more and save more money. Missions now cost $400 per month—is that a lot? Yep. Show your parents you love them. Work as much as you can and try to pay for some of your mission; it will mean a lot once you're out here.

5. Spend as much time as possible with your family! As much as you think it will happen, your girlfriend won't be the one writing the most letters to

you! Your parents and siblings are the ones who care and matter most. All the strength and energy you receive on your mission will be from them! It's true.

6. Exercise your priesthood. In the MTC and on your mission, you'll be called upon many times to give priesthood blessings to others. Do you know the sacrament prayers? The baptismal prayer? How to bless children, the sick, the dying? How do you consecrate oil? Do you know how to bestow the Holy Ghost on a person and confirm him or her a member of the Church? Can you confer the priesthood upon someone and ordain him to a specific office? So many words, and they are all important! Be ready. I've been in all these situations.

7. Be in shape! You know those jokes about elders missing buses and having to run for them? Well, it happens. Plus, you have thirty minutes of scheduled daily workout time in the field; be ready, cuz it's rad!

8. Know how to cook. Sorry to disappoint you, but frozen burritos do not exist in Europe. Ask your mom to teach you how to make a few simple meals.

You can get really tired of eating the same thing every day.

9. Do you know how to iron your own clothes? Wash clothes? This is something simple, but something that must be done. It's great back home how clothes just seem to wash themselves, isn't it? Do a few loads of wash this week, but limit yourself. Don't kill your mom by surprising her to death!

10. Learn to be humble. I entered the MTC somewhat confident. I knew the scriptures well and thought I had everything I needed, a testimony included. I was quickly humbled when I discovered I did not know the gospel as well as I should and that I did not know the scriptures as well as others. To top it off, I had to learn, study, and teach in a foreign language. Learn and know humility, cuz it will fall upon each of you.

And now I, Elder Cortney, do end my epistle. There is really no better way to prepare yourself for a mission than by choosing the right and continuing to do what you are doing as a faithful member of the Church. A mission is the hardest, most rewarding thing ever! As you serve, you will grow and be blessed enormously, as will your family members. I love you, and I love this gospel. Christ is my Savior; I look to Him; I love Him! Without the restored gospel of Jesus Christ we have nothing—with it . . . we have everything! The Church is true!

Sincerely,

Elder Cortney Lee Mathews

15

"My Attitude Now Is to Serve"

STEVEN TORRANCE
Mission unidentified

Hello, family of mine!

Can I even tell you the amazing thing that happened this week? It was so cool. I don't even have words to describe it.

A couple in our ward, both nineteen years old, have an almost two-year-old daughter who is blind, deaf, and paralyzed from the neck down. This little family was sealed in the temple on Thursday. Elder Kerr sealed them, but, I don't know, the things he said and promised them and blessed them with were amazing. The Spirit was so strong almost everyone in the sealing room was crying. That by far was the best part of my week; it was so indescribably amazing.

Speaking of the temple, we gave the Marcos family (who we baptized a few weeks back) a picture of the temple to put up in their house. Sister Marcos loved it. So the next time we went back to see them, it was up on the wall, in a kind of tattered, crooked little frame, but the best that she had. And, I don't know, it was so cool; their house just seemed a little cleaner, a little nicer. There was definitely a spirit there that wasn't there before—all because of having a picture of the temple on their wall. They are doing great and are so excited for the day they can go to the temple. I get so happy and excited for them when we go over there. It's so cool to watch them progress.

There are a bunch of times in my life when I remember doing things because I had to or with a bad attitude. I now think of what I missed out on because of my attitude. My attitude now is to serve and do what I am asked, and do so happily and gratefully. I have seen it work in my life and on my mission. I see it every day. Thank you all so much for everything; you are a constant example to me. I love you all!

Your son,
Elder Steven Torrance

PART 3

FAR FROM HOME

*"The keys of the kingdom of God are committed
unto man on the earth, and from thence shall the gospel roll
forth unto the ends of the earth, as the stone which is cut
out of the mountain without hands shall roll forth,
until it has filled the whole earth."*
—*D&C 65:2*

In order for the gospel to fill the whole earth, many
missionaries must travel to completely unfamiliar
surroundings, acclimating to new cultures, customs,
even foods. Part of the miracle of the missionary
experience is that they make that transition so
effectively.

16

"The Other Side of the World"

JOSHUA SCOTT
Russia Yekaterinburg Mission

Hey, family,

I'm in Russia now. It's hard to believe. Well, where do I start? I am in this cyber cafe above a shopping center right now. The keyboard is in Russian, so ignore any of my mistakes. It is so crazy here. I don't know how to describe it. It is basically the most ghetto place ever. Wow. I thought China was bad; I had no idea.

We left Denver and headed to Germany. I slept most of the way, and the flight went quick. We switched planes in Germany and headed to Ekat. As we were descending into Ekat, the pilot told us they were doing controlled burns in the land next to the airport and not to be alarmed. As we dropped beneath the clouds, all we saw was this raging fire. The vegetation on both sides of the runway was engulfed in huge flames. I felt as though we were flying into hell, because that is sure what it looked like. But we landed fine and then jumped off the plane (literally) and got into a big cold bus for the ride to the terminal. There were only two planes in the whole airport.

The entire terminal was no bigger than a stake center. We all went through customs without any problem and found the APs and mission president and his wife waiting there for us. We loaded into this huge van and headed to the mission home. We were only about fifteen minutes into the trip when the van broke down. The driver said that was normal and got out to try and fix it. We were parked in the middle of the freeway basically, but our president's wife said to not worry because there was nothing to be intimidated by. Just as she said that, three big Russian tanks rumbled by on the freeway. I was thinking to myself, What have I gotten myself into? All the new missionaries were freaking out. We finally got to the mission home and crashed. It was so nice to sleep. And the next day and a half was all just orientation stuff.

I got assigned to the city of Pervoralsk, which is located about forty-five minutes northeast of Ekat. There are just four missionaries in my district, and the other two live another hour away. That's four missionaries for 250,000+ people! We obviously have lots of work to do. Our area is on fire, though. We teach more discussions than all the other areas. I have already taught five in about two days of real work. It's crazy. There are thirty members in the branch, but only about nine are active. But there were fourteen at church on Sunday. We have church in the plant storage room of a big cultural center. It's a really trashy room, but it works.

People love to mess with us here. In fact, we had to stop wearing our name tags this past week because of problems with the *"riveatti,"* little street gangs. The last couple of days have also been holidays, so everyone is especially drunk. Most people are drunk all the time, anyway, but even more so on holidays. People stop us and ask for money all the time. All the time! Most people are jerks to us, but some are really nice too.

This has been a very humbling week for me. No

matter how confident I felt about my Russian leaving the MTC, I really know nothing. It's tough (really tough) to have to totally depend on someone else when it comes to such everyday things, and I desperately want to wake up one morning and be able to understand everything everyone is saying. But that's not going to happen. I have already started to buckle down with my studying, though.

The Church is true. Even in Russia—especially in Russia! I hardly ever feel homesick because nothing reminds me of home. Everything is so different. This has been a tough last couple days, but I knew they would be. Attitude is everything. If I can keep a good attitude, the language will come, my confidence will grow, and I'll be able to be the missionary I want to be.

Our apartment is on the seventh floor above this bank. Sounds nice, huh? But you should see the bank. We have three bedrooms, a kitchen, and then two things that can partially be classified as a bathtub and toilet. For baths, I crawl into this tub about half the size of an American tub and douse myself with a hose. Literally, a hose. We do have running water, but it is either scalding hot or ice cold. There is nothing in the middle. I don't even want to try to explain the toilet. Trust me, it's bad. Water here is also bad. We have filters, but they only work if we have water to put through them. We have like no water pressure at night, so we get most of our water in the mornings. We eat good here. We get about $200 U.S. a month for all our food, etc., per missionary. That's about four times what a whole Russian family lives on. We eat like kings and live like serfs. Such is life. It's my life now. I have so much to say and so little time to say it.

Well, I have to go. I am doing all right; well, I am alive at least. I'm finally on my real mission. Hard to believe, I know. It's tough, but then again I never expected it to be easy. Love you all. From the other side of the world.

Love,
Josh

17

"'Count Your Blessings'"

J'LENE FERNANDEZ
Paraguay Asuncion North Mission

Hola mama y papa (y todos),

I have two stories to tell—one is worldly and the other is not.

The worldly: Today I was able to go with the elders of my district to *el central* and to a mall. It was weird because for two hours it was like I was in the U.S. It was a major change from what I am used to here in Mariano Roque Alonso. I saw Lancome and Christian Dior products! My companion and I walked into the fragrance store and sprayed ourselves with expensive perfume. There was actually real air-conditioning! The clothes were so nice, but very worldly. When we walked back outside it was like, oh, yeah, I'm in Paraguay. The good part was that we ate at McDonald's!

The spiritual: The area in which we are working

has both middle class (which would be the poor in the U.S.) and poor rural areas (which would be deep poverty in the U.S.). The other day we went to visit a member who lives in one of the poorest areas and who has six children. This *hermana* lives in a house that is about the size of my bedroom at home. The house is made of rough wood and has no bathroom. But this sister is someone we all can learn from because when we asked her to pick her favorite hymn for us to sing, she chose "Count Your Blessings"! I'm learning so much from these people. I'm so grateful to be here. It is truly a blessing for me.

The children on the dirt streets run barefoot. Seeing them reminds me of the Christian "Save the Children" commercials on TV, but you know what? These kids have no idea they are poor! They run and play with their dogs, laughing happily as they kick their half-inflated soccer balls. I wish you could be here to see it. I love to stop and talk to them. Some get so excited when they see us coming.

I love and miss you all very much!

Love,
tu hija linda

18

"Here I Am in Mexico"

NATHAN BERG
Mexico Mexico City East Mission

Dear Family,

Well, here I am in Mexico. This first week is something I will never forget. My first impression when I saw Mexico City from the plane was that it wasn't very big. I could just see miles and miles of tiny cinder-block shacks. I couldn't see the downtown. But, it turns out, this place is huge.

The traffic here is something you'd have to see to believe. Stoplights don't exist. They just put speed bumps everywhere so you have to occasionally slow down. Ninety percent of the cars here are old VW bugs and used taxis. You want to have a good scare? Try riding in a taxi in this city. It's amazing how people drive. There is no such thing as pedestrians having the right of way, and if someplace is big enough to fit a car through, you can drive there. We ride the taxis all the time, so I am pretty much used to it. It's truly crazy, though.

There are dogs everywhere, and I mean everywhere! Old skinny, sick dogs with all their fur falling off. It's crazy, the population of stray dogs. I already have lost some weight, so that is a good thing. We pretty much have only one meal per day, at two o'clock with a member. That's the main meal, and the rest of the time we are working. I never could have imagined how much work is really involved in being on a mission. I truly think we average about ten miles per day walking—no joke.

There are so many people who are ready to hear the gospel. The goal for our mission this month is to have three hundred baptisms—that's twice the average per month. This mission is the smallest mission in the world, geographically, but has the most baptisms.

My first area is called La Perla. Drive over to the dump and imagine building a city there. That's what it's like. There is a constant smell of garbage, but I am pretty much used to it now. It is also the highest baptizing area in the mission, and I know why now. The people are so poor and humble and ready to teach. We already have seven investigators with a baptismal date set—some for this Sunday and some for next. Exciting!

Well, I hope all is well with you, and I miss you a ton.

Elder Berg

19

"Everyone Had Lost Everything"

NATHAN TODD THACKER
Mission unidentified

Background: This letter was written by a missionary after he had served those who were affected by the tsunami in Indonesia.

Family:

Well, first and foremost, since ya'll asked about what happened down south, I will try to gather my thoughts and write it to you as best as I can.

Thursday night we got on a tour bus and left at 8:00 o'clock. We got into Pang Ngaa around seven or eight in the morning. The most gorgeous scenery I have seen in my entire life passed by as we were going through the small mountain ranges, seeing glimpses of the ocean off and on through all of it.

I expected to show up and see the damage immediately, but we went to a camp. It was just rows and rows of small pup tents and some rows of wooden houses they have started to construct for people to stay in.

One of the first families we talked to spoke only the southern dialect, so I had a fun time trying to keep up, but as I calmed down and just listened, the Lord blessed me and I didn't have too hard a time understanding. I am a true believer in the gift of tongues and the gift of the interpretation of tongues.

Everyone I talked to had lost everything—their homes and, most of them, their places of work as well. Many of them still had their motorcycles because that is what they used to escape the flood. Several of the people I talked to had put their families of five to seven people on their single 125 cc motorcycles. One father said he has no clue how he, his wife, and five kids ever fit on their tiny motorcycle. He doesn't think that he could ever do it again, but they all made it out alive.

I met a large extended family of fifteen to twenty people all huddled together underneath a canopy. They all just joked around with us and said that there is no use in being all upset over the whole thing be-cause they just have to move on and keep going. One of the brothers in the family told us how when the wave came, he had taken his seventy-plus-year-old mother in his arms like a baby and just run. He kept saying that even with this old lady in his arms, he figured he could have outrun the Olympic athletes. The great thing about this family was that they had been in a bit of a family feud, and the ordeal had brought them all back together and under one tent—just as happy as when they had been kids. They said, "If nothing else, at least we all love each other."

I met one lady where I just had to force myself not to start bawling as I talked to her. She told me that when the wave started coming, she grabbed her three-year-old son and her eleven-month-old son but just couldn't get out of the way in time. Her two children were ripped out of her arms. She just cried. I asked her if she had any hope left, and she said, "Not really, I can't even find their bodies." The notice on her door (they all have signs on their doors with an address and list of missing immediate family members) stated that she also had an eight-year-old son, and I asked if he had died as well and she said no. He was not home when it hit, so he was fine. She then told me that for the sake of her boy and his future, she needed to go on and get over it.

We then talked a little about the fact that her

two children who died are now in a better place because they weren't old enough to really commit a sin, and she took a lot of comfort in that. We discussed the importance of making a record of their lives and this whole experience so that she would always remember them. And even more than that, so her future children would know what their older brothers were like and what the tsunami was like.

It was good to talk to her, even though my heart really broke for her and I had a very hard time controlling my emotions. I met another father who had lost his eight-year-old son. All of this made me think of how much I love my family and the fact that I have no clue what I would do without all of you.

The stake president shared an experience with me that really hit home. He said he was talking to a woman and that she told him her husband works in Phuket, an island just off the coast. He was working when the tsunami hit, and he ran inland to safety. As soon as he possibly could, he called his wife from his cell phone and told her to get herself and the kids to higher ground because a tidal wave was coming and he had just barely escaped it. So she grabbed her kids and told her neighbors the same thing, but they all just laughed at her. They said that nothing like that had ever happened there and that she was crazy.

Well, most of those she tried to warn died. But her family is still here—no material possessions left—but she didn't seem to mind too much because they were all alive.

The stake president related that family's experience to the gospel and to the Second Coming and reminded us how we each have an obligation to warn our neighbors (made me think of D&C 88:81).

As we were leaving Pang Ngaa, we took a longer way around to see some of the damage that had occurred. I was shocked. When we got semi-close to the shoreline, all was gone. Everything was destroyed three or four miles in from the beach. It was all just washed away. Only a few houses were left standing, and they weren't inhabitable by any means.

Well, I love you guys a whole lot. I really, really, really do love you all.

Elder Nathan Todd Thacker

20

"I Am in Rajahmundry"

MICHAEL PAUL WALLACE

India Bangalore Mission

Background: The India Bangalore Mission covers all of India and also the country of Nepal. There are only sixty missionaries serving there. Of these, fifteen are elders from North America; the rest are natives from India. Missionaries have been proselytizing in India for just two years; prior to that, India was classified as a humanitarian mission. India has forty official languages and about one thousand other dialects. Currently, missionaries are teaching only in the English language. During these first three months, Elder Wallace was serving in Rajahmundry, where the dominant language is Telegu.

Hey, family and friends!

Well, I am finally here in India. I am sitting in this totally ghetto computer place; it is 500 degrees outside, and this computer is soooo slow. I am in Rajahmundry, a very dirty town next to a huge river.

I had to take a nineteen-hour train ride to get here from Bangalore, two days after my twenty-six hours of travel to India. I am not a fan of the curry, which is what most people eat here. I am already feeling sick every so often, but I am having fun!

The food isn't too bad because I can get corn flakes and lots of fruit and some other edible stuff. It is quite fun preaching the gospel, even though I sweat constantly while riding my bike (the only district in India with bikes), so much that I have to drink about four to five liters (about one gallon) of water a day. We sometimes have to teach in little hut-type things while sitting on the floor. There are no traffic rules here; everyone goes where they please, but mostly they do drive on the left side of the road.

The branch of the Church is fairly small but quite strong, and many members help us teach. The building is very nice, but the foundation has shifted so they have to do some kind of work on it; I don't know to what extent yet. I am really enjoying preaching the gospel and am learning to love the country and the people. Last week we had seventeen investigators. The members are awesome here! Here in RJY they are justly famous for good members.

I have seen my first cockroach, rat, and monkey, and I have been here only a week! Once, while we were buying fruit, a guy on a motorcycle pulled up next to us, and he had a bird in a plastic bag hanging off the handlebars! Maybe tonight's dinner . . . ?

Ever heard of elephantiasis? I have seen it, and it is so sad. There are cows everywhere, eating garbage, and wandering wherever they want. The sewers are open and run right next to the street. This is also one of the hottest places in the world!!! Fifty degrees Celsius in summer (120+ F.)—ugh.

I got hit by a lemon while riding on my bike! I have been persecuted for the Lord's sake! Okay, it was only a two-year-old who threw it, but still . . .

I love and miss you all. My testimony is expanding fast. I am working hard.

Love,
Elder Mike Wallace

21

"I Have Made Them Smile"

DEVIN BELNAP

South Africa Johannesburg Mission

Background note from Elder Belnap's mother: This letter was written after my son had been serving for just over one year. It describes his feelings for the people in South Africa after learning to know and love them. Of special note is that he was very ill at this time with mononucleosis, a chronic viral infection. Shortly after Devin sent us this e-mail, his mission president was instructed by missionary medical advisers in Salt Lake City to send Devin home. That broke everyone's heart—my son's, his mission president's, those of the missionaries in his zone, and those of the people in his beloved Tembisa Branch. After a sleepless night, the mission president called Salt Lake City again and got permission to keep my son in the country, on the condition that he be allowed to recuperate in the mission president's home, with supervision. This he did. Within ten days, after the prayers and fasting of many people (including, as Devin wrote, "the mammas of Tembisa in three different languages"), he was well enough and his blood tests were normal so that he was transferred to Soweto to continue his mission.

Dear Family,

Being a missionary in South Africa has changed my life forever. I literally won't ever be the same person again. Because of the things that have happened to me on a daily basis, I have had an awakening to the suffering of the South Africans. Each morning when I drive into Tembisa, I am met by a shack town or "squatta kamp," which is so large and the shacks so close together that you don't know where one ends and the other begins. I see people dying from diseases such as AIDS, elephantiasis, and even gingivitis. In other words, I see people suffering, children who are hungry and dying. I teach people who are also suffering.

While I was teaching a man who is suffering from gunshot wounds received in the past month, I felt an overwhelming feeling that the things I am doing as a missionary represent Jesus Christ in every way. Every day I have experiences, such as seeing an old woman or a suffering child on the side of the road, who do not understand a word of English, but I say to them in Zulu, "You are a child of God. He loves you. Good-bye." There is nothing more I can do for them. I am helpless and it hurts. I now have a better understanding of the Sermon on the Mount and the teachings of the Savior, "Blessed are the poor in spirit. . . ."

But when I was teaching Njabulu, I recognized an overwhelming whispering of the Spirit—that I am doing a great service to these people, even if they go unconverted and don't understand. I have spoken to them and said hello and have been kind and expressed a true love for them in the height of their afflictions and suffering. Most importantly, I have made them smile. Each night now—and I am sure I will for the rest of my life—I pray for these people, that Heavenly Father will ease their pain and suffering.

Please pray for me to get better. I am very sick with an infection. I just have to get better.

> Love you all,
> Elder Belnap

PART 4

A GOD OF MIRACLES

"And he said, Behold, I make a covenant: before all thy people I will do marvels, such as have not been done in all the earth, nor in any nation: and all the people among which thou art shall see the work of the Lord."
—*Exodus 34:10*

One of the great blessings of being a missionary is the chance to witness the Lord's hand at work. Whether they come in the form of divine guidance to knock on a certain door, priesthood blessings of physical healing, or manifestations of the Spirit to sincere investigators, miracles abound in the field.

22

"He Started to Hum the Melody"

BRANDON TINGLE
Argentina Cordoba Mission

Hi, fam,

I had a really special experience this past week. I hope y'all don't mind me sharing it. Last transfer we met this really great guy named Arturo. He is a really intelligent guy and really sincere. We gave him the first discussion and a Book of Mormon, with an assignment to read Alma 32. Before we left him, we set up an appointment to come back.

We came back, and he told us he had read all of that chapter, and then had started from the beginning and read like ten chapters of 1 Nephi—not only read, but took notes and marked good scriptures and had really good questions. My comp and I were so impressed with this guy's determination and sincerity to find the truth. We taught him the second discussion and invited him to attend church.

Arturo came to church, and we told him we would come by that day or the next. We went back Monday. All we intended to do was see how he was doing and answer any questions he might have. We got there and sat down and told him that if he had any questions we would try to answer them.

He said, "Yes, I have a question: Can the Lord answer prayers in dreams?"

My comp said, "Yes, he can, but you have to be careful because it can be just a regular dream or it can be from Satan. The Spirit always has to confirm it."

He said, "Okay," and my comp went on talking about something else. He then said, "Can I share something with you?"

We said, "Sure, go ahead."

Now, y'all have to understand something about this man. Before we met him, he had never set foot inside of a Mormon church or known any Mormons or anything. The only thing he knew about

Mormons was that the missionaries wore white shirts and ties and rode bikes.

Anyway, he told us that before he went to bed the night before, he had said a short, simple, but sincere prayer, asking the Lord to tell him if this was the true church. That night he had had a dream. He said, "In this dream I saw a couple of things, and I can't explain them, so I'll draw them." He went on to draw the Angel Moroni and the Salt Lake Temple. We had never shown him or told him anything about either one. He said, "In the dream I was in the air—high in the air. I was overlooking this structure" (the Salt Lake Temple). He said that he heard music and saw a huge pipe organ. He couldn't understand the words being sung, but when he started to hum the melody he had heard, and my companion and I started to sing "Secret Prayer," he began to cry. My comp and I were in tears already. He asked us how this was possible. We told him it was an answer to his prayers.

This story may sound weird or strange, but the Spirit was very strong while we were talking to him. I know that the Lord answered his prayer. After we left his house, my comp said that in the twenty months that he has been out here, never has he felt the Spirit so strong in a discussion.

Yesterday, we went to talk to Arturo again. Since that earlier visit about three days ago, he has read the entire *For the Strength of Youth* pamphlet and is done with 2 Nephi and has also quit drinking and smoking. He told us that he wants to be baptized! I have witnessed a rare miracle.

I am so grateful for the power of prayer. It has changed this man's life and has given me an undoubting testimony of it.

Love,
Brandon

23

"She Could Feel Him Healing Her"

JEREMY MAUGHAN

Louisiana Baton Rouge Mission

Dear Family:

I will just start this letter off by saying that everything is going great. This has been probably the greatest week of my mission.

We progressed an older lady through all six discussions last week, and she is scheduled for baptism this Saturday. She is seventy-three years old, and her name is Celeste Hart. She is awesome. She has a powerful testimony of the gospel. She loves the Book of Mormon and has even been finding people for us to teach. She is very excited to be baptized this Saturday.

The only problem is that she is very sick and can't sit in church for more than an hour, but according to D&C 20:37 she totally qualifies for baptism. She is sick with hepatitis C, which I guess is a terminal disease that has no cure. Well, if there was ever any doubt that she should be baptized, in my mind it was all taken away last Sunday. That evening we went to her house to finish teaching her the rest of the discussions. During the lesson, she bore her testimony to us about the Book of Mormon, Joseph Smith, the Savior, and the Holy Spirit. She understands it all.

Then we felt impressed to teach her about priesthood blessings, which we did. She said that she would like one and had even been thinking about asking us about something like that. She hadn't brought it up because she was afraid that we would think she was crazy. But she asked that we give her a blessing. So we said a prayer to bring the Spirit in, and, boy, was it there. My companion did the anointing, and I had the wonderful opportunity to give her the blessing. It was awesome. The Lord promised her some pretty powerful things in that blessing—things I would not have ever dared promise a person as sick as she is. The best promise was when I told her in the name of Jesus Christ that she would be healed.

After the blessing was over we were all kind of overwhelmed. She was in tears and was clutching her chest. At first, I thought she might be having a heart attack. Then she told us that she could feel Him healing her, and that her chest was on fire. It was so awesome. Since then she has continued to look better and feel better. She has more faith than anyone that I have ever met, and it was a night I will never forget.

So I have to say, even though I was not happy about coming here at first, it has truly been an answer to my prayers to finish my mission off strong. The Church is true!!!!!

Love,
Jer

24

"That Scripture Was Fulfilled for Me"

JOSHUA SCOTT

Russia Yekaterinburg Mission

Hey, family,

I had a cool experience yesterday. During lunch I was looking at this little book that I had brought with me that had information about the beliefs of other religions and compares them to ours. It was really interesting, and I found myself wrapped up in it. I read almost the whole book.

We went to English class last night, and one of our new investigators was there. For some reason, she was the only one in my particular class, and we started to talk about religion. This woman has a friend who is a member of another church, and her friend had told her that her friend's church and the Mormon Church were basically the same church. Upon hearing this, the woman in my class became very disinterested in learning more about our church. She asked many questions about our beliefs and the beliefs of the other church. I wouldn't have had any idea how to respond if I had not spent an hour reading about them just a couple of hours earlier. Not only was I able to clear up the differences between our two churches, but I was able to explain some of the similarities between the two religions and also explain many common grounds that our church has with her own Orthodox church. This completely changed her attitude toward our church and made her want to learn more.

After English class, we went over to her house and had a really good discussion. She is now a very promising investigator. The Lord has promised us in D&C 84:85 that "it shall be given you in the very hour that portion that shall be meted unto every man." That scripture was fulfilled to the fullest extent yesterday for me. The Spirit entered into my mind and told me to read this little book, without me even knowing it. Man, this gospel is true.

Josh

25

"An Older Man Wearing Glasses"

BRAD TAGGART

Paraguay Asuncion Mission

What's up, all?

This week went great. A lot of progress. The kid that was supposed to get baptized last week didn't get baptized. But he will get baptized this week, along with another lady, we hope. Other than that, we had nineteen investigators who came out to church yesterday. Out of those, about fifteen will be baptized this next month or in July. Cool, huh?

I had another amazing experience this week with somebody receiving an answer to her prayer. We have this family we are teaching, and one of the daughters has lots of doubts about the Church. We have explained to her that she needs to ask God, and we've promised her that He will give her an answer. So she prayed and asked for an answer. When she came to church on Sunday, we asked her if she had received an answer to her prayer. She told us that she had had a dream of an older man wearing glasses, and that he told her that he taught the truth.

She was telling us this just as we walked by a photo of President Hinckley. She looked at it and said, "Hey, that's him. That's the man I saw in my dream!" The Spirit was so strong that we invited her to get baptized, and she said yes.

It's incredible how God works. I love watching the miracles. Pray for us. We will be inviting lots of people to get baptized this week. It should be really cool.

I love you all. Keep truckin'.

Love,
Elder Taggart

26

"His Dad Came to Him in a Dream"

DANE STEWART

Germany Berlin Mission

Dear Family,

This week we had a really cool experience. We taught an older, really religious guy who doesn't have a church, but he got a Book of Mormon from a friend ten years ago. He knows it's true and knows it very well, too. He's probably read it more often than the average Mormon. A few years ago, his dad came to him in a dream and told him he had to open up a church here in Jena (right now we have to go to a city forty minutes away to church). And this guy is really smart, rich, and cool, and is definitely capable of being a bishop. So when we committed him to be baptized at the first appointment, he said, "Yeah."

Then we talked about how he can be sealed to

his parents. We told him the reason why his dad came to him in a dream was so that he could receive the necessary ordinances. He loves it. He even started crying. He can't stop reading Church literature. It's so cool because this guy will lead the Church here in Jena, which is exactly what we have been praying for. Yesterday my comp talked to him on the phone, and he put it on speaker phone, and all I heard was, "I am convinced that this is the truth!" Cool, huh? Look up Alma 26:16.

Elder Stewart

27

"He Began to Believe"

BRANDON TINGLE
Argentina Cordoba Mission

Dear Family,

I had a good experience last week. We have this one investigator whose name is Esteban. He is one of those people who never had the time or beliefs for a church. He's a really temporal kind of person. Anyway, he is about sixty-five and has problems with his heart and was not expected to live much longer. We started to teach him, and he began to believe what we were teaching. One day, he wasn't doing so good physically; in fact, he couldn't get out of his bed. So we went in his room to teach him. At the end of the lesson we asked him if there was anything we could do for him. And he said, "Yes, you can pray for me." We then told him about the blessing of the sick with the oil and all, and he said that he would like a blessing.

So we gave him one: I did the oil, and my comp did the blessing. When we were finished, Esteban didn't say anything for at least a minute. We just kind of stood there waiting for him to say something. He got kind of teary-eyed after a minute or so and simply said, "Thank you." We set up another time to return and teach him and then said good-bye.

A few days later we went to visit him. He invited us in; he was walking around with no problems. He told us that after we left that night he felt really good, in fact, a lot better! The next day he went to the doctor for a checkup, and the doctor told him, "Esteban, I don't know what happened, but you don't have the same problem anymore." He then diagnosed Esteban with a different, less serious problem and gave him some medicine that will take care of it. Again, the Lord has blessed me with another great experience.

Love y'all,
Brandon

28

"'Be Still, My Soul'"

SEAN STEWART
Korea Taejon Mission

Dear family,

Hello, how are you doing? I'm really good.

Sunday was a really cool day. Pak Dae-Ho, my investigator who will receive baptism, came to church, and he wore his suit this time. Man, he looked so good. It was so cool. He walked into the chapel in his suit, said "Hi" to me, and kept right on walking to talk to some members, and that was so cool. If you ask why, it's because at first the missionaries are the investigator's only friends, but then what happens when they transfer? The new members go inactive if they don't have other friends. So it was so cool that he felt comfortable with the members.

Looking at him in his suit and everything, I almost started to cry.

We had a great experience the other day. A member lady invited us to her house. She is one of the strongest members, but her husband is not a member, and she has a teenage son who is really struggling. He is inactive, comes every once in a while to sacrament meeting, but that is about all. We went to her house, ate really well, and then we were going to have family home evening. I picked the opening hymn, "Be Still, My Soul," and Elder Black said it was one of his favorite songs too. Then he told us why. In one of his other areas he knew a family where the wife had been diagnosed with cancer. She had a husband and five kids. She had to go up to Seoul to take tests to see if she really had cancer, and while they were waiting for the results, their youngest daughter, who was only two years old, started to sing that song. She sang all three verses. Her father asked where she had learned the words, and she said an angel had whispered it in her ear. Later, the cancer tests came back positive, and the mother died a few months ago.

Elder Black finished telling us this story, then we sang the hymn, and then ended up just singing different hymns all night. Then we had to go, and the mother said that every room we go in there is a special spirit there, so she asked if we could say the closing prayer in her son's room, the one who is really struggling and who wasn't home. We did, and because our president told us to bless all the houses we go in, we blessed her son's room through the priesthood. The boy's mother was crying when we were done.

It was a really cool night.

Anyway, I've got to go. We're going to visit a member's husband in the hospital. Hope you all are doing good.

Love,
Elder Stewart

29

"I See Miracles Every Day"

ISAAC TRUMBO
China Hong Kong Mission

Hello, everyone!

It's been raining here for the last week or so. There have been thunderstorms and harsh wind, but not a typhoon yet. Whenever it is not raining, it is hot and humid. But I love the weather! I don't care if it is hot or cold, raining or snowing, the weather is always good.

The work is going forward as always, always picking up as I go along. I see miracles every single day! The other day, a member from DaiPo called me. He said that he was working in MongKok and had found a place where a lot of Mandarins lived. We went with him, and he guided us into the heart of MongKok. We went into this hard-to-spot outbuilding and walked up to the eighth floor. It was a place a missionary could probably never find on his/her own.

We knocked and asked if we could come in. It was kind of a boarding house for workers who come down from the mainland. They come and stay for about three months and then go back. Well, I sat there talking to a twenty-year-old man who had zero idea who Jesus Christ was, or anything even close to religion. But in ten minutes, with a lot of help from the Spirit, I got him really excited and interested to hear the lessons and come to church. He was also urged to bring some friends. It was great! After he is baptized, and his family and friends are all members, and he is a bishop up in China, I bet he is going to look back to that day and wonder how we ever found him on the top floor of an eight-floor building in the middle of literally hundreds of others.

I know that Heavenly Father is gathering the elect to build the kingdom of God in this area. And now we know where to go to get a constant source of new investigators and baptisms! I'll tell you how it turns out.

Another miracle happened yesterday. My

companion was at the church on exchanges when a man walked into the building. He said he needed someone to be a witness. He and his fiancée had just come down from the mainland to be married, and they needed two citizens to witness his marriage. Well, they talked to him, and he was incredible. He had met with the missionaries when he was in Hong Kong years before. After they taught him the discussion, he wanted to be baptized and was anxious for him and his wife to be married in the temple as soon as they have been married a full year. Well, they are married civilly now and said they will come to church on Sunday. It shouldn't be too long until he is baptized.

I could go on like this forever. We see miracles like this all the time! It is incredible. We are teaching more than ever before. And we are baptizing more than ever. I really am being blessed.

I love you all,
Elder Isaac Trumbo

30

"'Hey, You're the Mormons'"

ADDISON WELCH

Louisiana Baton Rouge Mission

Family:

Hey, it's been a great week here. I hope the same for everything there!

The coolest thing happened, probably the most cool thing yet. We chose a street on the map and prayed about it and prayed that the Lord would prepare someone for baptism on that street, and then we tracted it full of faith. This was yesterday in the biggest rainstorm so far (so we were soaking), and it was in a rich area. In the first few houses, the people were way mean and stood there and yelled at us. One lady threatened to call the cops. She slammed the door, and we went on.

Well, that lady followed us in her car and stopped us and said the cops were on her cell phone. We just kept tracting, and she followed us in her car—she even got out and went ahead of us, knocking on doors, telling the people the cops were after us. So we decided to go back and get our bikes and start from the other side of the street. I was scared of the lady—but still we prayed that we would find that person whom the Lord had prepared.

On our way back to the bikes, a man driving by in a car stopped, and the man asked if we needed a ride somewhere. We said, "No, we're on bikes." He said, "I live on this street. Come get out of the rain a bit." So we rode over to his house and taught him. As we were teaching him, we saw the lady still going up and down the street in her car, looking for us. I believe we were being hidden from her by the Lord.

Well, this guy wasn't interested, and we left. We still hadn't found the person yet.

We went to the other side of the street. Four doors down was the biggest, nicest house on the street, and we knocked. When a man answered the door, he said, "Hey, you're the Mormons. Come on in!" It was a black family who had just moved from California. It was the son who greeted us. He's in his

forties. He told us he had met with missionaries before in California. I asked what they taught him, and
he said family history work, and he showed us all this
genealogy he had already done. We started bearing
testimony of how families can be together forever,
and he said, "Yeah, that's another thing. I need you
to prepare me for baptism, so I can do my ancestors'
work in the temple and get sealed to my family forever."

We were stunned and speechless. The Lord really
did answer our prayer. He tested our faith and then
blessed us.

I know this is the one and only true gospel on
the face of the whole earth. I'm so thankful that
families can be together forever. Most people here
believe that, but they don't know how it works and
that their churches don't teach that, which is sad.

I love you, I love you, I love you.

Love,
Add

PART 5

TRIALS OF OUR FAITH

"I cried by reason of mine affliction unto the Lord, and he heard me."
—*Jonah 2:2*

Missionaries grow in all kinds of ways. But sometimes the greatest growth comes after their faith has been tried.

31

"Hidden Messages of Love"

Mission unidentified

Dear Family:

I am in big trouble. I still feel like a greenie and no one believes me anymore. They expect me to know how to do things. I have learned a lot. More than I can put in words. I believe I am truly beginning to understand what it means to work with all your soul, heart, might, and mind. I hardly sleep anymore but talk with God all night, pouring out my soul unto Him. When I finally sleep, I dream of the work, putting the thoughts of my heart into the *charlas* in a way I am not able to do in the conscious world. I plan every minute of my day and exhaust all my strength. I have lost all reserve.

I remember things from my childhood that apply to the Lord's investigators. Last week a man asked me when I first knew that God loved me, to which I responded, "As far back as I can remember." I told him about a time when I was very young and Dad was mowing the lawn. I was mowing the lawn beside him with a bubble-blowing toy mower. I remember that Dad picked me up and put me on his shoulders, and I remember how happy I was. I told the man that I felt the same way when I was baptized and that I feel the same way now. I know that God loves me.

I think trials and tests are hidden messages of love. People who know me a little more personally know a few of the trials I have gone through and ask me how I keep smiling. I tell them that my mother says I have always smiled since my youth up. I tell them that they would smile, too, if they knew where their trials were taking them. Sometimes I am so happy I just laugh! I can't keep it in. It just strikes me as so funny that as far as the world is concerned I have nothing but the clothes on my back and yet I am so rich!

My patriarchal blessing says that the Lord will bless me with powers that I never thought I would have. I was fourteen then; now I am a twenty-year-old missionary who can testify that the Lord keeps His promises. I have seen and heard and done things that I never thought I would or could see and do.

I love you all and pray that the Lord supports you in your trials. Just trust Him. I close with a scripture that reminds me of my life, "I have written according to the best of my knowledge, by saying that the time passed away with us, and also our lives passed away like as it were unto us a dream" (Jacob 7:26). Life is a dream! A great dream! May we live it well so that in the last day we may awake to the glory of our Father and abide in the full light of His eternal love!

> Your brother and son,
> Elder Leavitt

32

"Singing Hymns in the Dark"

AUTHOR'S NAME WITHHELD
Texas Dallas Mission

Dear Mom and Dad:

Another P-day has gone the way of all good P-days. We got up early to play tennis. I thought we were doing pretty good; then these two twelve-year-old girls came up and were playing in the court next to us and made us look ridiculous. Big fat embarrassment. After the match, we were talking to them and their dads. When we told them we were missionaries, one of the girls said she hoped we were better missionaries than we are tennis players.

We set a goal to tract for thirty hours this week and were six hours short, so we decided we would tract for part of our P-day to make it up, so we tracted from 3:00 until 9:00. No one wanted to talk to us. Everyone seemed really rude. I don't know why, but sometimes it's just like that. One guy yelled at us for playing with his garden hose—said we had messed with it and made it leak. Then it started to rain. When we got home, one of our investigators was waiting for us. She said she had talked to her husband and that she couldn't see us anymore. She said she really liked us and she hoped we weren't mad but that it would be best if we didn't come back again. I can't tell you how bad it made me feel. She was one of the sweetest ladies I have ever met. It broke my heart. I don't think we'll ever see her again.

When we walked into the apartment we were so bummed, we didn't even turn on the lights. We just lay on our beds, not saying anything, kind of staring up at the dark. It was really raining hard by then, though the thunder had quit, and the rain was pounding on our old roof. We have a leak in the hallway, and it started to drip.

Then Elder Marshall started to sing. He started singing "Because I Have Been Given Much." We ended up singing hymns in the dark for an hour or so.

I think I will always remember that rainy night, singing hymns in the dark.

Despite everything, it turned out to be a good day.

33

"I Felt Your Love"

CHASE GUNNELL

Ukraine Kyiv Mission

Background note from Elder Gunnell's father: My son's best friend is his older sister Dayna. When Chase left for his mission, he knew that Dayna would probably get married while he was gone. Sure enough, it happened. He always said that the day she got married would be the best and most successful day he would have on his mission because he would be where he was supposed to be, serving the Lord. We received this letter right after her marriage.

Dear Family,

I have to admit, I was really excited to read your letters this week. I have been wondering how everything went this past weekend. I am glad to hear that everything turned out wonderful. I didn't expect anything less, but as always, it is nice to have confirmation.

Anyway . . . about our week. First of all, I have to say that Saturday was probably the hardest day I have had on a mission yet. I knew it would be difficult because Dayna and Nate were getting married, but it surpassed everything that I ever imagined. It was difficult. I was sad about not being home, but I was determined to work hard and prove why I was out on a mission. My whole mission I have prayed to Heavenly Father to prepare someone for me on that day because that was the day that I was going to "prove myself."

On Saturday, the people seemed meaner than ever. I have never had anyone yell at me more than they did on Saturday. We also couldn't get anything started. We did a lot of contacting, stop-bys, tried to set up discussions, but to no avail. I was getting discouraged because we couldn't do anything. It was terrible.

Then at about seven at night, I finally went into a room and prayed. I asked Heavenly Father if I was doing everything I needed to, to find that person He was preparing. I asked Him why the people were so mean to me and if there was something more I needed to do. Then I received an answer that I wasn't expecting, but it comforted me, and I think you would like to hear it. First of all, I felt your love. It was such a wonderful feeling. It was just like I was at home crying and having my family there hugging and comforting me. It was such a wonderful feeling. Thank you so much.

Then, that love moved to the love of my Heavenly Father. As you all know, that is such a wonderful feeling and always has the answer. The answer that I received was, "Chase, I have prepared a person today, and that person is you. You said that this is the day that you would show your love to me, and I was testing you to see if you really do love me, and you passed. Thank you for your service."

After that I just started to cry, and my prayers were answered. I can't even begin to say how wonderful it felt. It was one of the most touching experiences of my life. I then went out, and the people that were yelling at me didn't bother me anymore. I knew that I was doing the will of the Lord. Thank you for your love and your prayers. I will always remember that day.

The next day Heavenly Father rewarded me openly. We had four investigators out at sacrament meeting, and something like that hasn't happened in this branch for about eight months. Also, we taught a few discussions to investigators who were really receptive. Then we added up our numbers for this week, and we had the best week that we have had together. We turned in the names of nine progressing investigators, which is really good for us. I loved it, and I am thankful for my Heavenly Father's love to me. I have come to have a testimony of the principle that we can never repay the Lord for all He has done for us. When we do the will of the Lord, He rewards us openly to the point where we will not have room enough to receive it. I love it.

I love you all. Thank you!

With love,
Elder Chase Gunnell

34

"You Guys Are Men of God"

AUTHOR'S NAME WITHHELD
Mission unidentified

To the Family:

Today it all came together. Everything. This has been a hard area. It nearly sent me home. The past two to three weeks especially. First, my mission president really reamed me in my personal president's interview. Then the assistants to the president came over in an exchange along with the zone leaders the day after, and then my district leader came to visit the day after that. Nobody in the streets bothers to listen, and I felt so alone. I was close to packing my bags and going home. Then, on Wednesday, I got food poisoning, and I was sick until Saturday. When I finally got enough strength to go back out and tract, we went to visit a stop-back.

This stop-back's name was Jimmy. When we met

him on the street, he was just heading in and didn't want to talk much because of the cold weather. We gave him a Book of Mormon and wished him the best of luck. That was about two weeks ago.

We knocked on his door and he answered. He remembered us and told us he had read the Book of Mormon twice through! I about fell over in shock. He also told us he believed it. We set up an appointment to meet with him Monday (today). When we went over there he had a fever and didn't want to meet. We asked him if we could do anything for him. He said, "Not unless you can lay your hands on my head and heal me in the name of Christ." Again, I about fell over in shock and said, "Would you like us to do that?" He said, "You can do that?" and we obliged after we explained the priesthood.

We went into his apartment, and he didn't have a chair. So instead he knelt down and Elder Dayton anointed him with the oil, and I gave him a blessing. After the blessing, he didn't immediately get up. He stayed on his knees for a few moments, and when he eventually arose with a tear-soaked face, he said to us, "I believe. You guys are men of God."

He later told us how he had been researching religions since the age of sixteen and hadn't found what he was looking for.

He said when he first met us, he knew our intentions were pure. And when he read the Book of Mormon, he knew it was the word of God.

This is why I have been tried. I know this church is Jesus Christ's church on the earth again. I know that because I've witnessed life without it. It's true and I am thankful. I love you guys.

35

"The Very Long Walk Home"

NATALIE WATTS
Zimbabwe Harare Mission

This week I had some interesting experiences but one defining moment in particular. On Thursday, Sister Dutiro and I got the inactive list from the Relief Society president and spent the day trying to find the inactive sisters. We both felt prompted to go to certain places, so we followed the Spirit and went—but had no success. It was a very frustrating day, full of "fall-throughs." As we started the very long walk home, I couldn't help but feel discouraged. The road kept getting longer and longer and my strength weaker and weaker. I thought, WHY? Why didn't things happen today? We followed the Spirit—but what good had it done? The conversation continued in my head:

Impression: "You were obedient, weren't you?"

Me: "Yes, but there were no results."

Impression: "So—why do you need results? Isn't it enough to have faith that you were in the right place at the right time?"

Me: "Yeah, I guess so—at least I know I can 'go and do.' But I am so tired! Was my effort really worth it?"

Impression: "Why did you get out of bed this morning? Why did you 'waste your energy' by being obedient?"

Me: "Because I love the Lord so much. But I will never be able to really show Him how much I love Him. I can't give enough. I can't believe I have to walk to Kamwala tomorrow. I don't have the strength! I love Heavenly Father, and I know He needs me to go down to Kamwala tomorrow, but I just can't!"

Needless to say, by then I was in tears. Then an image came to me of me kneeling at my Father in Heaven's feet, sobbing, saying, "I love you so much—but I don't have the ability to show that love. Whatever I give will never be enough!"

Then I saw the Savior kneeling next to me and heard Him say, "Father, I love her so much that whatever she can't give, I will make up. Please accept the offer."

One of Satan's greatest strategies is to make me think that the Atonement is only for big sinners—but people on the right path have to do it by themselves. I now have a real understanding of the Atonement of the Savior and how much strength I can and must gain from it.

We went to Kamwala the next day, and it was great. How thankful I am for the Atonement. How real it is! And it's not just a one-time-use thing. Strength comes daily, even hourly, from this precious gift. I know I will never have enough, but it's okay if I trust my Savior, Jesus Christ, to make up the difference.

Sister Watts

PART 6

WHY WE SERVE

*"For they were set to be a light unto the world,
and to be the saviors of men."*
—D&C 103:9

Why does the Lord ask our young men and young
women to serve missions? The answer becomes
clear to anyone who serves, as demonstrated in the
following stories.

36

"We Cried in Each Other's Arms"

JARED ERNI
Netherlands Antilles Mission

Dear Family,

I had a funny dream last night. It was so strange for me because all of a sudden I was in a farewell meeting before going home. People started coming in. As I watched the people coming in, most of them were missionaries who left the same time I did. Josh Horne walked in, and I ran to hug him. Dan Randolph also came and Matt Stafford, Ben Fulton, Chris Kidd, and other friends who had served honorable missions also joined me in this meeting. I was so happy, and I think it was a deep joy I felt not only because I could be with my friends but because we hadn't seen each other for two years while each of us was helping, working, and serving to bring souls to Christ.

At one point during the meeting, everyone started walking away. I began to follow, but for a second I turned back around. Tears filled my eyes because somehow I knew when I walked away, I wasn't going to be a full-time missionary in Holland anymore. I was leaving the country, people, and culture I have learned to love and serve. And I didn't know when I would be able to come back.

Josh dropped behind the crowd and put his arm around me. We cried in each other's arms for the people we loved and walked away together with teary eyes—knowing also we had done and completed the work the Lord had sent us to do.

I thought of Alma and the sons of Mosiah when I woke up; so I read their account in Alma 17:2, which says: "Alma did rejoice exceedingly to see his brethren; and what added more to his joy, they were still his brethren in the Lord; yea, and they had waxed strong in the knowledge of the truth; for they were men of a sound understanding and they had searched the scriptures diligently, that they might know the word of God."

After I had the dream, I bore my testimony in

my ward sacrament meeting. I felt I should share part of what I had dreamed, and it seemed to touch a lot of people, and I was able to express my gratitude to them by sharing this spiritual experience. After the meeting, two new people made appointments with us to be taught.

I love my family, and I am so thankful I can be with you forever.

Love,
Elder Jared Erni

37

"You're Here for Others"

SEAN STEWART

Korea Taejon Mission

Background: This letter was written by a missionary to his younger brother, who was leaving for his own mission in a few weeks.

Hey, so how you doing?

You're almost gone now, two weeks or something, and I'm excited for you. It's going to be so fun. You're going to make so many great friends, do so much good.

My comp and I were talking the other day, and he mentioned how he has such a long time to serve and how I have hardly any time left. He asked me if it really was the best two years of my life, and I said of course. Then he asked why. I had to think about it for a while. It was kind of a hard question to answer because it's hard to explain a mission. But I'll tell you, I have met a few people here who are so important to me that I wouldn't trade the chance of knowing them for anything in the world. And I mean that very literally. And I may never see many of these people again. Not in this life anyway.

But still, a mission is hard to explain. Of course there are hard times. But they are a different kind of hard because you aren't here for yourself. You're here for others, and so the hard times are going to be when you really love someone and you have something that can help them, but they won't listen. And how great is that, to be able to spend two years and not worry about yourself even once? I spent the first nineteen years of my life not caring about a single person but me. And how cool is it to spend two years not thinking of yourself at all?

And don't worry about whether you'll be able to help anybody. Just go and enjoy every second of it. Enjoy the hard times just as much as the good. When I first got here, I remember a missionary whose mission was over and he was bearing his last testimony before he went home. He was crying, and he said, "When I go home things will be good. They will be different, but still good; but as for this, right now, this is a moment I will never forget." That stuck with me for some reason, and I've tried to take advantage of the moments I'll never forget—like teaching investigators or visiting a member family that you are close with or watching someone's life change. So don't worry. Just like that scripture says, "Be still and know that I am God." Just learn to trust He knows what He's doing, and you will love your mission so much.

I love this work. I'm so glad for the chance I have had to be a part of it. If I could serve just one more year in this area, I'd do it in a heartbeat.

Never pass up a chance to bear your testimony of Christ because through bearing it, you find it, and it becomes a part of you. And through hearing it, others' lives are changed. Lose yourself in the work. You'll hear that many times, but when you finally do it, that's when the Lord can really use you.

Too bad I won't get to see you before you leave, but, hey, look on the bright side: I get to see the Korean rice fields planted one last time!

> Your brother,
> Elder Stewart

38

"The Only Source of Lasting Happiness"

TRENT WHITE

Brazil Campinas Mission

Background note from Elder White's father: Elder Trent White served in the Brazil Campinas Mission. His mother, my wife, Colleen, age forty-eight, fought breast cancer for five years and was taken off all medications and officially pronounced terminal by her doctor, with only one to two months to live. Elder White left for Brazil knowing he would never see his mother on earth again. This situation has produced many incredible and emotionally difficult moments that have also produced much faith and eternal thinking.

Only Colleen, Trent, and I were at home when I gave him a father's blessing before we left for the airport and his departure, and that started the tears flowing all around. Trent brought out his violin just before we left and played "Families Can Be Together Forever" for his mom. It was a sweet and loving act on his part. Afterwards he hugged and thanked her for guiding him from an early age to learn that musical instrument so well.

At the airport, Trent's three brothers handled the good-bye hugs pretty well, and I did pretty well with just a tear or two. But when it came time for Trent to say good-bye to his mom, it was just heart-wrenching. I had not really thought about that moment until it occurred, even though we had talked much about him leaving and the permanence of it to Colleen. All the intense feelings of sincere motherly love and their final earthly parting, absent a miracle, just over-whelmed them as they hugged and hugged, and wept, and hugged again. If ever a mother loved her son, and a son loved his mom, it was genuinely displayed for all to see at that moment.

Such a wonderful thing to behold, but such a heavy price to have to pay!

The following letter was written by Elder White and read during his mother's funeral service:

To Family and Friends:

Even though I am far distant from you this day, I do not feel it. Although I have been greatly com-forted because of your prayers in my behalf and the blessing of the Lord, I join with you in my intense feelings of loss, gratitude, and hope. Let me briefly speak about each of these.

Loss: On April 7, 2005, our world, our community, and our home lost a precious woman—my mother. I have come to appreciate and love her more and more over the years, and especially during the last year when I have been with her and without her. I've come to find that the mere thought of her fills my soul with warmth and makes me want to be a better person. To speak of her is for me a sacred thing, for she exemplifies our Savior so well. All who have known her have felt of her great love that she so freely gave. Although I've lost her for the rest of my days in this mortal life—and what a great loss that is—my memory of her will never cease to guide me.

Gratitude: Never in my life have I felt such gratitude to my Heavenly Father. Only the Savior's love for us, as demonstrated in His atoning sacrifice, exceeds the love of my mother. I will forever be grateful for her. To be brief: she gave me life, she raised me up, she loved me unconditionally, and she let me accept the gospel of Jesus Christ for myself. The worst thing we could possibly do in this time of mourning is to not give thanks for the privilege of having Colleen White in our presence and in our lives.

Hope: In my preparations here at the São Paulo Brazil Missionary Training Center, I study, learn, and prepare to teach the plan of salvation. This is the message my mom wants all to hear and believe.

To that end, I would like to explain again why I will not be coming home for the funeral. It is Jesus Christ Himself who has called me to be His servant here in Brazil. I have not felt the responsibilities, or blessings, of this calling ease one bit with the passing of my mother. But I have felt the strong and compassionate arms of our loving Savior supporting me and carrying me as I have and continue to fulfill my labors in His ever-so-important work—that of bringing souls unto Him, who is the only source of lasting happiness, even our Savior, Jesus Christ.

> With great love,
> Elder Trent White

39

"What Now?"

AUTHOR'S NAME WITHHELD
Mission unidentified

Dear family:

This is the last night of my mission. Tomorrow I come home, and this will be my last e-mail from the mission field.

I keep asking myself, can this actually be real?

Oh, wow! It was everything I could have asked for. It is so sweet, the way I feel right now. I feel as though two years ago I left home to come on my mission, and now I am leaving my family to go back to Utah. These people here are my family now, in so many ways.

For the first time in my life, I feel completely satisfied. It is so good to take these people you love so much and tell them how much you care for them. All I want is to be with them.

I simply can't believe this is over. I don't even know what to think. There is so much to say and no way to say it. I know that God has sanctified me because I have been willing to serve. I know I have done what God has asked me to do. I was called to serve, but everything I gave up was so inconsequential compared to what I've been given in return.

What can I say? I'm so happy. I'm just so happy. I wish I could take this moment and these feelings and make them last forever. I'm so sad to leave. I want to come home and see you all, but I don't want to leave these people or these feelings.

But I know that I have to.

All day long, the same thought has been running around and around in my head:

Well, God, what now?

40

"The Holy Ghost Confirms It"

SUMMER BARRICK

Brazil Manaus Mission

Dear family,

And now I'm here at the mission home. My bags still aren't packed—think that's gonna have to wait until tomorrow.

So what do I say to end this, the last e-mail? My thoughts are "Thanks!" Thanks to you all for your love and support and e-mails and everything. Thanks to all the friends I have here. But mostly, thanks to my Heavenly Father and my Savior for letting me have this wonderful privilege of being a missionary.

I know that not everyone gets to do this, and not everyone gets to finish. I almost didn't. But I'm going to. And for that, I will be forever grateful. I am grateful also for the lessons learned and for the changes that I have seen in the lives of others, as well as those in my own.

I know God is our Eternal Father and Jesus Christ is our Savior. The Lord truly paid for our sins and died on the cross so that we can live again with Heavenly Father. And that's why He organized His Church—to teach us about what He did and what we must do to return to Their presence. Joseph Smith was called of God to restore this gospel and organize Christ's Church once again. The men in this church have the priesthood, the power of God, the authority from God to act in His name. We know all the saving ordinances that must take place here on this earth. Families can be together forever. The Book of Mormon proves it all, and the Holy Ghost confirms it in my heart. I know these things to be true; I know it more than I know myself. God loves us. He sent His Son to die for us. And I will do all He asks so that I can see Him one day again.

I love you all so much. Thanks again for everything. I'm so excited to see everyone.

> I love you, I love you, I love you,
> Sister Barrick